F
B

ALSO BY DOUGLAS KEARNEY

Someone Took They Tongues.
Mess and Mess and
Patter
The Black Automaton
Fear, Some

BUCK STUDIES

design by Douglas Kearney
text in Janson Text; titles/subtitles in Tw Cen MT and Futura
published in the United States by Fence Books
Science Library, 320
University at Albany
1400 Washington Avenue
Albany, NY 12222
www.fenceportal.org

distributed by Small Press Distribution and Consortium

Library of Congress Cataloguing in Publication Data

Kearney, Douglas [1974–]
Buck Studies/Douglas Kearney

Library of Congress Control Number: 2016951784
ISBN-13 978-0-9864373-7-3   first edition
10 9 8 7 6 5 4 3 2

BUCK STUDIES

douglas kearney
fence books, albany, ny

TABLE OF CONTENTS

Ecce Cuniculus

No Wake/Too Much of Fucking Everything

Headnote to a Done Poem

Notes and Acknowledgments

this one's for you! (uh-uh!)
this one's for who?
us! us! us!

— Petey Pablo
"Raise Up (All Cities Remix)"

Stagger Put Work In

1. Herakles
    Greek badman
some say
    was for killing kin
compelled to do 12 Labors

                    didn't he

flay the Nemean Lion
    slay the Lernean Hydra
hound the Ceryneian Hind   *didn't he*
    bind the Erymanthian Boar
scour the Augean Stables
    expel Stymphalian Fowl   *didn't he*
grapple the Cretan Bull
    break the Man-eating Mares
take Hippolyta's Girdle[1]   *didn't he*
    steal Geryon's Cattle
pluck the Hesperidean Apples &
    abduct plutonian Cerberus   *didn't he*

2. Stagger Lee
    Black badman
some say
    shot Blackfolk by the paddy'ful
shot the high sheriff & his honor
    shot the hangman & the Devil

but near all say Stagger
    shot Billy Lyons[2] dead

                didn't he
                didn't he
                didn't he
                didn't he
                didn't he

---

[1] Most tellings go that though Hippolyta was willing to give Herakles her war-belt, Hera tricked the Amazons into fighting him and his men. He killed Hippolyta in combat.

[2] An exception of note: "Stagger and Billy," one of two versions of the story Tina Turner recorded. In this take, Stagger Lee flirts with Billy's wife and Billy beats him severely. Ike Turner—Tina's then-husband—penned the lyric.

MANE

bad Stagger Lee's bad song a cathoused toast bout killing some cat.
Stagger bad Lee's hard bad rock song bang Lyons a wet hole,
body him with a shot's heat.

    Stagger put work in,
      Billy got worked. gunned down Billy
Lyons' dead song falsetto the saloon. *please don't take—*.

    what a man what a mighty badman.

    Lee as some Herakles! Herakles!

Herakles the badman kill the lion.
skin him for to wear him.
Stagger wore Lyons out.

seem some cats see Lyons anywhere but mirrors,
where, lying, many wear Stagger's smokehouse lips,
take his song up our mouths,

    a badman's tongue,
    a slick low note.

no doubt
he make something out us.

NECKS

and know he love it, the badman, from jump.
bust-off one head come two to lay down.
    again and over.
       each damp stub jut to cherry vipers
stiff then limp, slip and twist of muscle twitch throat-deep
and bang lips open.
Stagger, braggart lover, can dagger for hours,
till cock-hollered crack of dawn.

       love all that cut-up, two new holes to tell it: *Stagger!*
Stagger! figure Lee chop till Monday, week after?
Billy knocked again and over,
too quick he drop, eager lover.
can the bad bad bad bad stay up till summer, winter?

pow come two new mouths to fill with red tune.
each new hole gape then pucker
then blossom unpopped mambas. *Stagger!*
    Stagger! pow off his senseless hips
    again and over.
bang bang summer after next till ever
   and *Stagger!* the hard dark heat busting new skulls:
a song this wound turned mouth—the badman—
       won't know to stop.

SHOT

so winter melt when Herakles buck her dear down
and the unplucked huntress grit her red-eyed ololyga
to bring us back to doe sprung up.

to hunters, prey precious:
a gangsta's nada sans mark-ass.
weird mirror, blood.
what would Stagger call himself minus Lyons lying
on the wood floor? who'd call him?

Artemis speak her burst hart back to quick,
a soundboothed gangsta say
    that shit hot! run that shit back!
so BOOM   CLAP   ʙᴏᴏᴍ BOOM   CLAP
    "shot that boy so bad…
      broke the bartender's glass":
made a gang of little mirrors. Billy! Billy! Billy!
who sing a Billy back
      from the bucking   "shot that boy"
     for Stag to buck him back? "shot that boy"
                    "shot that boy"
go BOOM   CLAP   ʙᴏᴏᴍ BOOM   CLAP
  hot!
     run that shit back!

ROOTER

pigs prey to piggishnesses. get ate from rooter to tooter.
I'm a hog for you baby, I can't get enough go the wolfish crooner.
the gust buffeted porker roll in the hay
or laid down in twig rapine. let me in, let me in.

    no drum-gut, Stagger's stomach a tenement:
his deadeye bigger than his brick house.
Stagger Lee live by the want and die by the noose,
whose greedy void's like a whorehouse
    full of getting full. won't get enough!
rumored Stagger'd root through pussy
to plumb a fat boy. here piggy! whatever
Lee see he seize: whoever. know how he do it:
manful (to?), ham-fisted. sorry Billy,
    us made your name "Mud" and who dig dirt like swine?
they get in it like a straw house. Lee got down.
Lee get dirty.

SHIT

but what's too much of shit peel our stink eye.

that nigger ain't shit, so us don't give a shit
bout that piece of shit getting shot. make it go way.

what's gone is dead and what been dead deader now,
just a stank mound of did and done once gone scudding down
    a hunger's black river.

     LYONS   ... *my life!*
     US   fuck that shit, nigger!

like, Stagger, this Billy business
some business, this mess
some mess. make it go way.

yoke the mitt your pistol ride in on and till.
you could could you crook Jordan, make the Mighty Muddy lean
with just your trigger finger's black hook?

make it go way. over that black-ass shit,
       gently shirr—o Stagger—
                your blues cold and sure.
make the shit done and did, then gone.
it reek with what us don't want keeping.

iron tune, trill, cut the tongue to song.
    thrill the singer's heart, balloon
the chest. red breast.

bulletproof song, balloonskin singer —
            the tune scores and clefts.
all the little birds' cast iron beaks.
        pop the singer red-breasted.
        pop can't kill the song.
                it cut the tongue
but not off. all the little balloonskin birds
thrill in the bullet song. Stagger song. red.
            red. bullet scores. clefts.
Stagger can't kill the song.
Stagger song pop.
        all the little singers' hearts trill.
        all the little hearts aren't iron. bulletproof
breast, the tune thrill
        but can't kill. the tongue,
        red. the beak
cut and cast the singer Stagger.
            Stagger can't kill all the little birds.
pop. song can't kill all the little pop birds
        pop. the cleft.
            the cleft hearts. the red breast—

BULLY

and a live nigger just a past due sacrifice like a bull too pretty to die.
bully Stagger's longhorn brimspan and oxblood crown crown him
    bad bad bad bad and bull.

only good one dead one us(?) scold our mirror. should've been dead
before Stagger rassled it bull-headed red-blind muscle-a-muscle.

bully and bull stagger the city levee round round round.
who say: let's walk down
and china shop the Hellenic Belluthahatchie,
cut antic in antiquity's Diddy Wah Diddy,
     ATHENS ST. LOUIS CAIRO KANSAS CITY?
they pretty beefcake too fine to die but is that the goddamn gods'
    damn rules?
       fuck them all.
or whose work to be did and Stagger put it in: heeeere Billy!
bully Lee's bully bullet bully Billy lay by bull Lee by and by biddy
    bye bye.

who say: *let's run down*
     MEMPHIS CHICAGO SPARTA DETROIT
only good nigger Lyons. Billy loin, rump none too pretty beefsteak.
Stagger, bull too pretty to ride the slab but
stagger round round round red-blind with work to be did: since.
     and fuck one of em.
should've been rassled before he deaded Lyons,
swear us(?) seen for what bull the bull-headed headed.

   God clutch his steak knife like a lightning!

see, badmen ate by what's between their legs.
so a plug cranes a veiny neck to that *whoa*-ing sugar cube stack,
chew to a red of prairie.

      gun a stunt cock for rough stuff. Stagger go down
  into his junk,
    skeet into Lyons. slung slug some slag-cum-spunk.
Billy bellow a birthing yelp
and stagger, Lee sprung out the stunt cunt he fix in him.
smoking pistol his papa. muzzle flash umbilical.

Stagger dick won't take *whoa* no more so
    "Stagger..." "Stack-o-..." "Stago-..."
  give dim hard-ons mouths.

pianola a doula. Stetson bassinet.

    "Stagger..." "Stack-o-..." "Stago-..."

mare and red prairie, horseflies
  ride the bloody muzzle and bit.
saddle and bridle fall like belts, flies.
    as so the broken break *whoa*
               then go on to break. so
    blood on the broke oat stalk.
    blood on the broke hat.
    blood on the slave's cutlet lips—
a dick eats its mister, still working the reins.

peach job and clover. figure:
"damn, at last 'proper' cockwork."
fetching porte-jarretelles off fetching Amazons:
ham-gammed, yam-chested.
      skiff-stiff to Pleasure Isle, wang
          dang doodle. do Stagger's shitty hard-leg ditty
need kitty kitty?
sure, his main thang undo her belt for to spring
the bad bad bad bad out sing-sing,
but he got no love for her whom he tools
      and he been in the bing where it ain't
          no fun (to?) if Hippolyta down for it!
mad madam Hera hear Herakles' rap—
cockblock peace;
got beef's rocks-off,
brick houses cut mighty mighty broad,
our hero's gory fist
      grip ripped trim. "thin" line between love
          and hate that hard for a man
seem a love? to? Stagger, asshole, say "wait a second. shit!"—
Stagger's asshole-print hancock say: "danger." to?
read it undercover: love letter—to?!—
as lipstick on a pillow.
undoing's Stagger's argot,
      sweet zero: when the slugs penetrate you
          feel a burning sensation below my belt
when the screen read rough. *a hound's sound. for? a warning, a surrender.*
      danger; I love you. *what's this*

strange relationship? Billy snatch
Stagger's hat. "don't play with me, boy.
give it to me." six gun cum. Stagger hung,
                    their striptease end bloody.
what to call this:
        rough?
        thin line? undone belt;
        cocked strap?
                "don't mess with me,
                boy—"

HERD

still the thunder of Stagger's hips steal Thunder's thunder.
his hips' steel: supercell black till it thunder slug heat, bone white.

    Power to the Stagger us singsong sifting brown sugar
      from shit and back.
what stink so good about Stagger? his rap sheet of stiffs?
how he do prod the herd with uncut don't-give-a-fuck?
his hot monogram red as shepherds?
how that hardrock cowpoke make himself himself's own stallion
and ride—whoa!
    Stagger to the People!

now tomorrow come over some shot-prone pussy set to weep
for his now herdless field blank as a shorn cheek.
turn shorewards, simp! see the sea abet a badman's stealing.
shifty thief in its ancient gray hood, its in-out.
Stagger spur his mount,
yaaaaaah, cut a rut down the littoral. *yaaaaaah!*
    is *Power* Lee there to rustle us off to greener?
boom go Thunder or Stagger or breakers
though us told us hear our Collective Hoof.
boohoohoo go the wounded herdsman, slapfaced
while a new name burn to smolder black in our skin.
over and again.

FRUIT
Billy as Atlas speaks

"say I trade this weight for what and gate-hop to runagate delight,
surrender to some better shoulder.
the badman gather damp palms, bungled muscle what I got,
bar the garden path to that fruit he after.
                 I'm soft as old apple,
my floppy meat slop off my lank flank.
rockhard, he out the chain link—
                           handles my shit with outlaw slackness.
I jack this orchard's gilt Delicious.
come to feel some lil bit swell
till he ask me take it back a sec,
and I recollect the dull pounds of boys
slugging lawns to corners—all us lit with June's cruel noons.

see I take it so he'll see I could.
malus I stole plump his bobbing back pocket, winnings.
he go out song like a damn planet humming,
he go out song like a gavel slamming…
summer pass blameless and dumb-assed to autumn,
         lousy with apples,
red as streetlamps to Hell
and all them screen doors riddled in little men.
I hold my shit like a wound."

MOUTH MOUTH MOUTH

Stagger get at the end dogged by the work.
he reckon by Billy's plot dug spade-dark—
that sorry-ass passage Stagger can't quite pass quiet—
under there's the Devil.

Stagger tics who he killed—a whorehouseful, a courthouseful—
but tilts his limp Stetson only at the Billies billeting yonder.
won't beware, just diddy on down:
under there's the Devil.

a bark, then a boom.

them stories always sortie a bad bad bad bad
to bum-rush a stingy hell
and heel back something savage on leash.

what's "always" but meaning to make a mountain
of a tune learned over and again?

suddenly: barking at the dark.

cats, us catch us cornered in our skin,
groins cocked at ourselves.

Stagger shatter that mirror then Stagger shoot Billy.
don't take my life! whose? who's
to say whether one blubbers *please*, or glowers *I can't go with that*
as the bad bad bad bad us had had swagger down into refraining?
under there's the Devil.

and when Billy peep Stagger stagger on and out,
to cell, to noose, to rule Hell's roost,
Billy get up get up get up get up to sweep
the pieces out like pine dust on a brothel's Monday dawn;
fixes to fix the glass
              as all the little Billies falsetto a song:

                    "he done me wrong"
                    "he done me wrong"
                    "he done me wrong"
                    "he done me wrong"

then   a bark.

again and over the cathouse doors swing wide,
in come a tongue-red hat. a wet thing stiffen behind our lying teeth.

That Loud-Assed Colored Silence

loud
|loud|

ADJECTIVE:
producing or capable of producing much noise;
easily audible:
they were kept awake by loud music | she had a loud voice.

• strong or emphatic in expression:
there were loud protests from the lumber barons.

• vulgarly obtrusive; flashy:
a man in a loud checked suit.

ADVERB
with a great deal of volume:
they shouted as loud as they could.

colored

| ˈkə lərd |

ADJECTIVE

1 having or having been given a color or colors, esp. as opposed to being black, white, or neutral: *brightly colored birds are easier to see* | [in combination] : *a peach-colored sofa.*

• imbued with an emotive or exaggerated quality: **highly colored** *examples were used by both sides.*

2 (also **Colored**) wholly or partly of nonwhite descent (now considered offensive in the US).

—OXFORD AMERICAN DICTIONARIES

Boom.
Clap.
Boom. Boom.
Clap.

Boomboom.
Clap.
Boom. Boom.
Clap.

Boom.
Clap.
Boom. Boom.
Clap.

Boomboom.
Clap.
Boom. Boom.
Cla

WEEEEEEEEEEEEEEEEEEEEEEEEEEEEEEEEEEEEEEEEEEEEEEEEEEEEEEEEEEEEEEEEEEEEE
EEEEEEEEEEEEEEEEEEEEEEEEEEEEEEEEEEEEEEEEEEEEEEEEEEEEEEEE
EEEEEEEEEEEEEEEEEEEEEEEEEEEEEEEEEEEEEEEEEEEEEEE
CLAP! EEEEEEEEEEEE CLAP! CLAP! EEE EE/EE
CLAP! EEEEE CLAP EEEEEEEEEEEEEEE EE/EE
CLAP! CLAP! CLAP! CLAP! CLAP! CLAP!
CLAP!CLAP! CLAP! Boom. Boom. CLAP!
CLAP!
...
...
...

....

         ... .

.... DON'T ....

....

.. *bluh-die cuh-dot* ... ...

.... **SCAT IS A SHITTY THING**

.....   **TO SAY. IT IS SHIT THAT FALLS**

....   **LANGUAGE DOWN.** ... .

....SAY.... *buh-dee cum-puh-heh-dit*

"if the tongue is a reed   ... . SHIT ....
the teeth're sheet music.   .... **TO BE SHIT** ... DON'T
show Them your score   ......I...... ....
of ...... mute ...... notes.   AIN'T...... ....
.... SAID... ....

QUOTE... ....   *ex-zep buhbuh-die*

.. **IS TO BE A SOMETHING** SHIT... ....

...ME......   ... .

....   **OF NOTHING.** .... YET ......

CUZ... .... I ....   "tuxedo   your   stance

.... AIN'T...   where   you're   wanted

....   and play yourself shut

... . *mub pub-mih-duh!* ...... the fuck before that mess ....SAID

.... mess Our dichty diction." ....

....

      ....SHIT.......

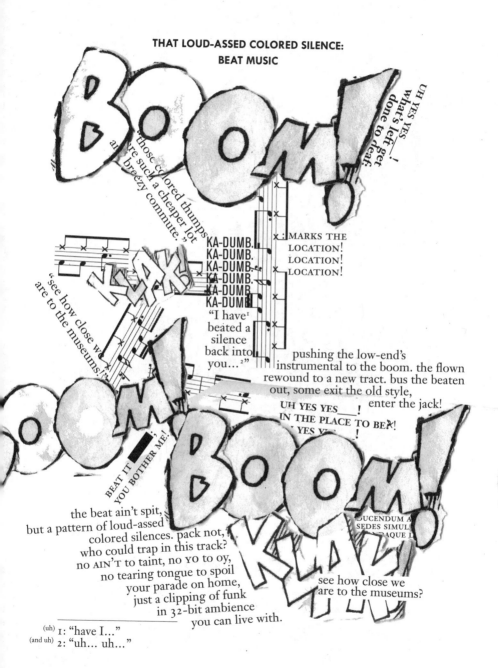

B O O M!

UH YES YES___!
what's left—
done to deaf.
get

"those colored thumps
are such a cheaper lot
a breezy commute."

KLAK!

KA-DUMB.
KA-DUMB.
KA-DUMB.
KA-DUMB.
KA-DUMB.
KA-DUMB

x : MARKS THE
LOCATION!
LOCATION!
LOCATION!

"I have[1]
beated a
silence
back into
you…[2]"

"see how close we
are to the museums?"

pushing the low-end's
instrumental to the boom. the flown
rewound to a new tract. bus the beaten
out, some exit the old style, enter the jack!

UH YES YES___!
IN THE PLACE TO BE !
YES Y___!

BOOM!

BEAT IT
YOU BOTHER ME!

KLAK!

the beat ain't spit,
but a pattern of loud-assed
colored silences. pack not,
who could trap in this track?
no AIN'T to taint, no YO to oy,
no tearing tongue to spoil
your parade on home,
just a clipping of funk
in 32-bit ambience
you can live with.

DUCENDUM A
SEDES SIMUL
AQUE L

see how close we
are to the museums?

(uh) 1: "have I…"
(and uh) 2: "uh… uh…"

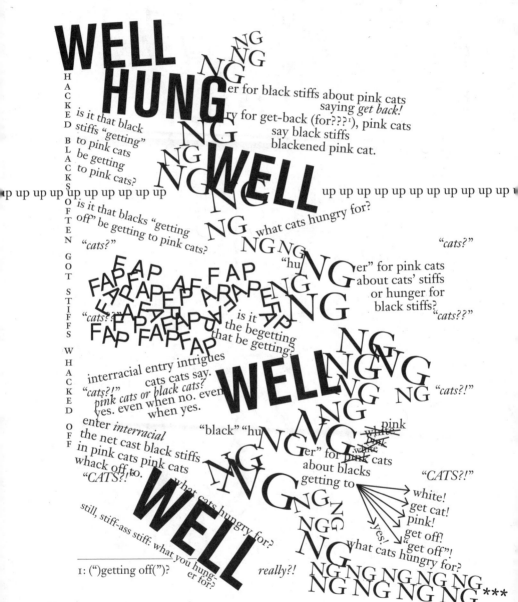

WELL HUNG NG NG NG NG NG NG NG NG NG **WELL**

er for black stiffs about pink cats
saying *get back!*
ry for get-back (for????¹), pink cats
say black stiffs
blackened pink cat.

HACKED BLACKS OFTEN GOT STIFFS WHACKED OFF

is it that black stiffs "getting" to pink cats be getting to pink cats?

up up up up up up up up up up

is it that blacks "getting off" be getting to pink cats?

what cats hungry for?

"cats?"

NG NG NG NG NG

"hu NG er" for pink cats about cats' stiffs or hunger for black stiffs?

"cats?"

"cats??"

FAP FAP FAP FAP AF FA PANG RAPENG FAP FAP

"cats?!" is it the begetting that be getting?

interracial entry intrigues
cats cats say.
"cats?!"
pink cats or *black cats?*
yes. even when no. even
when yes.

WELL NG NG NG NG NG NG

"cats?!"

enter *interracial*
the net cast black stiffs
in pink cats pink cats
whack off to.
"CATS?!"

"black" "hu NG er" for pink cats about blacks getting to

pink white wake

"CATS?!"

white!
get cat!
pink!
get off!
yes! & get off"!

WELL NG NG NG NG

still, stiff-ass stiff: what you hung. er for?

what cats hungry for?

what cats hungry for?

_____
1: (")getting off(")?

really?!

NG NG NG NG NG NG NG NG NG NG ***

broken black gone, broke to the canebrake?

get it?   get it!
get it!
get it?   get it?
get it?
get it? get it?
get it?get it! get it?
get it? get it? get it? the canebrake's english
'chu expect?!   get it! breaking brokered
a welwet coach   get it? get it?by the cane breaking open
for coonilingus?   get it? the broken's brains?
get it?.it?   get it!
get it?
get it? get it?
the black's broke english   get it! get it?
brooks break-ins   get it?
on the breakers' english   get it?   get it?
braking breakers' breaking.   get it!

what i say was i meant
what i had say was
what i meant when i say
what?

keen black   when do the fugitive
tongues keen   cold switch to f.u.gitive?
what they can ken,
canny. canines can't
get it! scan they lines through
tongues' fen. blacks break
for that great tungsten hung
up north, gone bog what   get it?
get it!   dogs them in the break.   get it!
open.

get it?
get it?

BREAK.

25

won't you let me take you on a ~~sea~~ cruise?

ROCKETS

TAKE ME TO ~~YOUR LEADER~~
TAKE ME TO ~~YOUR LEADER~~
TAKE ME TO ~~YOUR LEADER~~
TAKE ME TO ~~YOUR LEADER~~
TAKE ME TO ~~YOUR LEADER~~
TAKE ME TO ~~YOUR LEADER~~
TAKE ME TO ~~YOUR LEADER~~
TAKE ME TO ~~YOUR LEADER~~
TAKE ME TO ~~YOUR LEADER~~
TAKE ME TO ~~YOUR LEADER~~
TAKE ME TO ~~YOUR LEADER~~
TAKE ME TO ~~YOUR LEADER~~
TAKE ME TO ~~YOUR LEADER~~
TAKE ME TO ~~YOUR LEADER~~
TAKE ME TO ~~YOUR LEADER~~
TAKE ME TO ~~YOUR LEADER~~
TAKE ME TO ~~YOUR LEADER~~
TAKE ME TO ~~YOUR LEADER~~
TAKE ME TO ~~YOUR LEADER~~

so far ahead
it's behind us.
Moses tote her
raygun saying
moonwalk or git
disinigrated!

pharaohs go far away-o, no riding place down dere!

thrones thrown up like they just don't care!

[eject!]

what our antenna said we was bugged,
so us eyed the light up to light out.
whole of "...the place" blacked up so blacks out
this terra. o great gettin up launchin!
spacesuited Q.U.E.E.N.S. in foil to fly.
flightsuited kings sky around shinin.
zip zip zip off the planetation,
beyond the stairs to nigga heaven.
it's an escape craft
from now&then
by way of then&soon.

ROCKETS

TAKE ME TO ~~YOUR LEADER~~
TAKE ME TO ~~YOUR LEADER~~
TAKE ME TO ~~YOUR LEADER~~
TAKE ME TO ~~YOUR LEADER~~
TAKE ME TO ~~YOUR LEADER~~
TAKE ME TO ~~YOUR LEADER~~
TAKE ME TO ~~YOUR LEADER~~
TAKE ME TO ~~YOUR LEADER~~

MOONSHOTS

"yeahyeahyeahyeah"
"yeahyeahyeahyeah"

it's the Where,
the When we go
" when the Call
gets no Response.
[do you read?
over.]

who you callin BUCK Rogers?"

ASTROSHEEN®
REMY MARTIAN®
~~CADILLITE®~~
~~GADILACTIC®~~
SPACEY ADAMS®

TAKE ME TO ~~YOUR LEADER~~
TAKE ME TO ~~YOUR LEADER~~
TAKE ME TO ~~YOUR LEADER~~
TAKE ME TO ~~YOUR LEADER~~
TAKE ME TO ~~YOUR LEADER~~

"NASA been good to us!
Dogonnit, I'm serious!"

ROCKETS

MOONSHOTS

vaaeee-ooo!

are we *there* yet?
are we *we* yet?
are we *we* there?
are there *we* there yet?
are we here *yet* there?
there,   there.

who you callin StarBUCK?!"

"pilot...
"pilot...
"pilot...
"pilot...
"pilot...

THAT LOUD-ASSED COLORED SILENCE:
HUMAN BEATBOX

EPIGRAPH A ❏   EPIGRAPH B ❏   EPIGRAPH C ❏   EPIGRAPH D ❏

BEATIN UP THE BLOCK WITH
THE NOISE BROUGHT THE
MUSIC MADE MY SELF A COON-
TRAPTION
BO JUMBO WELCOME TO
THE JUNGLE BOOGIE!

SHUT YER TRAP.

SHUT YER TRAP.

MOUTH

DRUM-

beat yourself. up
jump de loogie
dat short the fuse
of machine to skin.
patterns spattttter
your soup coolers
to stoop woofers
for to oogabooga locution.

talking drum
become
drumming talk?

SHUT YO TRAP.

(A) *all the noise! noise!* —The Grinch
(B) *bring the noise!* —Public Enemy
(C) *a noisy noise annoys...* —Anonymous
(D) *...a joyful noise...* —Traditional

THAT LOUD-ASSED COLORED SILENCE:
MODERNISM

who among us has not
entertained a silence,

standing there loud-assed
and colored beside the white
chickens?

```
00 a   00 a
00 a   00 a
00 a   00 a
00 a   00 a
00 a   00 a
00 a   00 a
00 a   00 a
00 a   00 a
00 a   00 a
00 a   00 a
00 a   00 a
00 a   00 a
00 a   00 a
00 a   00 a
00 a   00 a
00
```

~~KAEK(RIK)A(N)
(MERKIN) BOP~~ AKA:
AKA: WOKE UP
THIS MORNIN
DA MYSTERY...

either to be good at the worst of the things
or a good one of the *worst* of things one could be.
at it. right right(?)(!) so to mean to be *bad*
at the worst of the things's good in the *worst* way
which is *bad* since it's bad to the "good" and thus good
to the *worst* of things one could be. at it.

I only been a good nigga
for a minute though...

too *bads* a positive
when times them times.
but time comes to right
the worst of the ways which is good
unless "good" since "good" sees the *bad*
as the bad. thus to be a "good" thing's
to see the *bad* thing as the worst of things,
which ain't no good.

I only been
a good nigga
for a minute though...

you know how I feel?
the light goes on !!!
for a darkness, I jet
as though dawned-up
to the illest sensation. I reach
the shit and feel me. I'm *at* it.

I only been a good nigga for a minute though...

da
dun
doooooooone.

MMMMMMMMMMMM
MMMMMMMMMMMMMM
MMMMMMMMMMMMMMM
MMMMMMMMMMMMMMMM
MMMMMMMMMMMMMMMM
MMMMMMMMMMMMMMMM
MMMMMMMMMMMMMMMM
MMMMMMMMMMMMMM
MMMMMMMMM

too bad for words.

NOT BAD MEANING BAD BUT
BAD MEANING

the truth is slap yo mama!

BAD MEANING BAD BUT
GOOD
MEANING BAD
MEANING GOOD

MMMMMMMMMMMMM
MMMMMMMMMMMMMM
MMMMMMMMMMMMMMM
MMMMMMMMMMMMMMM
MMMMMMMMMMMMMM
MMMMMMMMMMMMMM
MMMMMMMMMMMMMMMM
MMMMMMMMMMMMMMM
MMMMMMMMMMMMMMM
MMMMMMMMMMMMMMM
MMMMMMMMMMM

**YOUR MOUTH WANTS
TO DO SOME SHIT.** ## NOT BAD

MMMMMMMMMMMMMM
MMMMMMMMMMMMMM
MMMMMMMMMMMMMM
MMMMMMMMMMMMMM
MMMMMMMMMMMMMM
MMMMMMMMMMMMMM
MMMMMMMMMMMMMM
MMMMMMMMMMMMMM
MMMMMMMMMMMMMM
MMMMMMMMMMMMMM
MMMMMMMMMMMMMM

M god body embodied
embedded up in it
imbibed it feel the spirits
god **M** a body god up in it
good god all the time
M sometimes I just wanna
want it [woman ⎤ up in it
[man ⎥
M [landlord⎥
[Lord ⎦

M

M

BUT
what you want
is the want of it.
you want it so we
got it

got to give it up?
could be being all up in it
let's all up in it.

TRAIN IS A-COMING
TRAIN IS A-COMING OH YES!

LIVID ENTERTAINMENT PRESENTS
★PORNEGROPHY!★

XXX

THE CUMISTAD
NUT TURNER
TOUSSAINT BEND'OVERTURE
HARRIET BUTTMAN
MADAM B.J. COCK'ER
MARTIN LUTHER KING-SIZE JR
MALCUM XXX

XXX XXX

XXX XXX

FOR BDSM! ROUGH! EBONY!
MONSTER COCK! INTERRACIAL!
LOVERS

"love has nothing to do with it;
love has everything to do with it."

[SAFETY WORDS?]
TAKE IT! TAKE IT! TAKE IT!
TAKE IT! TAKE IT! TAKE IT!
TAKE IT! TAKE IT! TAKE IT!
TAKE IT! TAKE IT! TAKE IT!
TAKE IT! TAKE IT! TAKE IT!

}

whose
is this?! whose
is this?!

GIVE IT TO ME! GIVE IT TO
ME! GIVE IT TO ME! GIVE
IT TO ME! GIVE IT TO ME!
GIVE IT TO ME! GIVE IT TO
ME! GIVE IT TO ME! GIVE!

YOU *no!* want "it."

give it up?

slave asks master:
what's my name?
master asks slave:
what's my name?

whose
is this?! whose
is this?!

M: *can you take it?*

s: …

M: *all of it?*

s: *I can take it*

s: *"oh yes!"*

M: *do you want it?*

s: …

M: *do you want it?*

s: *enough.*

M: *not the safety word.*

M: …   s: *what's the safety word?*

how much too much how much
enough?
is much too much much?
is too much much?
how much too much much?

whose is this?!

give it up?

BETTER GET YOUR–

whose this is?!

BETTER GET YOUR–

OH–

The Black Woman's Tear Monger

they come dear, but go cheap.
they run clear, but flow deep.

THE BLACK WOMAN'S TEAR MONGER

STREET-CRY OF THE BLACK WOMAN'S TEAR MONGER

bright cities & towns, sun up & sun down
mongers-of-black-woman's-tears at hollering.
all the all the folk like shrikes a'cluck, "it's a 'lullabye'":

> *by the bottle! by the bucket!*
> *by the barrel, gotta go!*
> *by the sip or by the river,*
> *come and get a lotta more!*

'ADE

take your many of USAmericans, who
                                    (for that way-back body thirst)
        guzzle black women's tears
                                ahhhhhhhhhh   [...]
        & smack
        wet lips
                            aaaaaaaaaaaah   [!!!]

IN ORDER TO MAKE AN OMELET

are they to be gotten in cartons?
        bobbled black women's tears:

    shell
                or yolk,
        broke
                or loosed?

37

TV'd to the live evening lede:
black woman clipped to a moan of *gone*.
       LED'd against blackness streets, her tears
glint a plugged nickel jackpot.

STICK-&-MOVE

some men,
      but [tend-to-be] men,
           mistake black women's tears for speed bags—
{in this World(!) where these chains(!!) stay on we(!!!)} "thus:"
          —[tend-to-be] some men
      fight for right to what's wrong.

STREET-CRY OF THE BLACK WOMAN'S TEAR MONGER

more in stock
than that At-
uhLAAAAAAN -tic!
stock's on that At-
uhLAAAAAAN -tic!

KEEPING UP APPEARANCES (BIG PICTURE THINKING)

pale &
pale smog farts
Ol' Streetsweeper's rig, rinding grimy curb-bankments.

       city mended new pink
              & pink under scabs
what were black women's tears.

THE CARNIVALESQUE

a young black woman bound ribbons to them as confused balloons
   gone down.

THROUGH THE THIN WALLS

black neighborwoman: her tears are clear feathers.
        hant canaries crash
          —! the glass that's her face.

DIVINING

they hear a sahara, there,
of a black woman's laughter
& scowling, cop their dowsing rods.

STREET-CRY OF THE BLACK WOMAN'S TEAR MONGER

they come dear but go cheap!
they run clear but flow deep!

BROOM JUMPIN'

those whose knots he tied

then notted, black women—
their tears

—stones thrown at the bigger one.

THEIR MOST DESPERATE PLAN JUST MIGHT WORK!

ACT 2 in *BIG SUMMER ACTIONER*—
hunting ingredients for LAST-DITCH CURE.®

brightening
FALLEN OFFICER   I know how to get the tears!

THE DOGS

there's that black woman! her tears
dug themselves from her stung ducts,
spilled to the road, tails affixed, pulled
her by the eyes all over town, a pair
of mastiffs. among us shear clutchers, who'll ask if
she'd wish to be freed? what new beasts she'd shed...

SHUCK

so *nacreous(!)* the tears.

maybe that black woman's sternum's an oyster's umbo...?

NEOLIBERALISM

a bootstrapping black woman'd macerate hers in vinegar.
lambskin pliability's that right swipe for now's consumer likes.

STREET-CRY OF THE BLACK WOMAN'S TEAR MONGER

plenty by the kettle,
plenty by the pail!

drop it like it's hottentot venus.
dip   rump   other
trip   keister   **her** soot tinted skin
slip   **ends** up on tv.   dirt   rind
sink   video   soiled   husk
teeterin til tits up.hd   rotten. **hidin** pole.
drunken   on **dv** imprison in shot.   rod
tilted   onto   nut   penis
soused   **hip** to under.   spoo   tool
tore up the donk.   lesser   seep   I hit it. *provoked* to
            tush   vile   I **pour** it on. poke pushed to
            hind   spit   strike pressed to
look. nude **heinie**   shit up slot.   stroke driven to
peek   spoil   slit   *she* lust **prod** **onus** *hers*
peer   in the **stink.** repulse pit
see so rotund into   hole
    distort   inside   **kitten** to split.
    revise   **enter** the pink.   rip
    edit the pose. turn poon   sunder
hooker do sit n **spin** pivot tenders shred
                      tissue   rive
            she tripe**loin.**   rend
            nothin'   **rent** it out ho.
            nil   pro
            slop in skirt.   prostitute
                              she **isn't** loved
                                   no
                                   nope
                                   not
                                   never.

this black X-hat an ex-X-hat. this X-hat was on some next shit, had cats callin cats "Black" way back. w/ the snapback rocked backwards or the hat brim low as a casket lid or the fitted fixed, rocked cocked back like X got knocked.

cocked gat ex'd X. had him X-eyed & stretched, back snapped by the gat the black buck buckshot shot X out the pocket. *get your hands out—*! X'd out the black X. rocked him out the pocket. *get your hands out my pocket!*

get your hands off my black X-hat, cocky black cat, Lyons! cocky till that gat staggered that cat. Stagger made an ex-cat of Lyons. get your hand off my Stetson! gun left son undone like a snap back put a nigga head out.

nigga head out w/o an X-hat on a nigga head where the nigga head at? wearing the X-hat snapped niggas to "Blacks" like X. the X-hat made ex-niggas like X made ex-niggas till that nigga ex'd X: snapped back, sawed-offed in the Audubon, long gone & gone like those black X-hats, black. tilted brim, broke.

to Big Thicket a**KRAK**is a buckshot   to Big Thicket**KRAK**is a
stick broke**KRAK**headlights staggering home   the road kills
buck**KRAK**to Big Thicket we go we go to sticks   to stick bucks
hot   drink drink heads light   stagger
                                          ing the road long the trees
long the creek**KRAK**stick broke   light kills   we go we go to Big
Thicket to home on a kill   buckshot**KRAK**stag
                                        gered by drink   head
light to Big Thicket   buck on each pick-up   staggering
                                        what you

looking at
                the pick-up headlights long the road **KRAK**buck broke
KRAKthe white stick Big Thick
                        et long the trees long the
creek   drink staggered   broke white kill the buck staggering
home**KRAK**the trees pick up   we
                          go we go gone to Big Thicket
what you doing here buck
                      stick to home**KRAK**stick broke huffhuffgogo
white light break the trees   break for home long the road home
whites homing on we   huffhuffgogo buckshot **KRAKKRAK**
                                KRAKKRAK
we go we go gone   to Big Thicket long the Huff Creek the rushes
in the drink hot head whites
                          what you think you are   the boot   buck
huff**KRAK**huff**KRAK**is fists boots bone**KRAK**a stick broke   buck

stick in the rushes   buck back in the rushes   put them

                                                    back on   put
them back

        on   buck head in the rushes   what you think in
the rushes   put them

                    back on   put them back

                            on   to Big Thicket we
go to Huff Creek-head hot   we go to head   staggering long the
trees the staggered creek-head the rushes**KRAK**a stick broke the
creek breaks   the hot light   to Big Thicket we go we go gone

                                                    to
white huff to buckshot to long road home we go   we go we gone

                                                        to
Big Thicket to Huff Creek Road   of drunk pick-ups   road kill stag
gering bucks hot   drunk   head light rushes Huff Creek Road

                                                        pick-
up rushes drunk and screech

                        ing brakes   Huff Creek rode by drunk
and screeching whites

                    whatyouwhatyouwhatyou

                                    to Big Thicket we go
we go gone**KRAK**is a buck shot**KRAK**is fists boots bone**KRAK**the
road kills **KRAK**a broke stick long the staggered creek it go it go

                                                        on

NIGGAS BE WATCHING THE NEWS IN 2015, Y'ALL,

like to been grunted out that foul starfish into the john, dook!
        feeling a low way about it,
        clap some "would" to wood, a tack, all caps: a couplet, cant.
      it's *breathe*, not *breath*.

        pound a pound key with them brown thumbs, fam.
        then sung till nubbed wick of soot smokes,
        up come morning pour that hot lemon, that honey, honey.

like to been pushed out that funky red eye squish, homie,
        plopped atop a yard of sidewalk, uncurbed—

        bucking bean bags? rubber rounds? electric boogaloo, bro?
        wet the bandana you don't like the pepper, papa.
        milk, mild soap, Maaloxed water.

like to been plunked out that pink asterisk stank, boo-boo,
        screech these bald e's be eating *what*? nigga,
        niggas be watching News not tch *Wild Whatever*.
      so like fish splash of little rodents is that stank?
        a brick out that pink asterisk and you know we're used up
             of Kleenex!
        a Nike'll do. it'll do. chamomile, low window sill.

like to been born out that rank cornhole, gal,
      they say *what color?* squat. pinch, still here, woke!
      but we jump down hella good,
      gut get a magnesia about it when we search engine with
them black ass thumbs
      to tally, to strike those fours to distraction. woooooooooo!

      mourning with our minds' set on the slow, bent arc; 's'okay,
      no prob, St. Xanax!

like to been deuce-moved out that pee-yew chute, sis.
      when we look, we look moonward,
      that chute we shot out shuts its rosy fist,

      we splut on car hoods, on oxidized locks of stiff founders,
      boughs of old poplars, a rock by a waters of fat-ass bass,
      streets of certain cities they say wilds grow too close to,
      plastic bag coming for to carry.

2015? all over our eyes, shoeprints stay, y'all.

said *I died*, his game finger on the burning one.
try again, said I touching his shoulder.

then he was piked on spikes and said *I died*,

game finger on the stuck one.
you can do it, said I mussing low his brown merino.

said *I died again*, gaming finger on the shocked—

I'm tired of this and turns from the burning world
to run and jump in the high world—

such shining gems up that little sky—

runs, but then. said *I died*, touching the falling one.
I know you're gonna make it, said I. too long

since cutting, his shadow fade too thick. *o!* said *I died*,

gaming finger at the falling one.
said I, *son, maybe you should*—.

o! said *I died!* the falling one. *hon, you can't just keep on*—

said I. *o!* a pendulum pendulums. said *I died!*
game finger touching the gutted one. he needs a good

—*jumping and jumping* said I.

o! said *I died o!* the one who falls and burns,
gets cut down turns from —

I'm tired of this. son, run said I *or stop.*

THE BLACK WOMAN'S TEARS SWAP MEET IS OPEN EVERY DAY

some black women are my friends & their tears seem the hems
        of blue dresses.   I ball un-ball
my pocketed palms
       & think on stockings, bells.

among my students sometimes number black women —
I wish their tears were rungs; such desire may too be grease, though.

my mother's youngest sister's torn calendar tears,
      Mondays, Marches, 29^{THS}, '91s & '70s
till wicker bins choke, shredder hacks.

a couple of tears, middle sister pinches at her eye,
a black woman's spyglass. she peers
through the wide between her &.

my older cousins, black women, their tears are:
    (A)   fresh batteries in broken clocks
    (B)   ruined coin souvenirs
    (C)   wheatbread heels jim crowed in fridges
    (D)   what pitted the yellow linoleum thus

the black mother of the black woman who married me,
her tears're sunk ships:
coral polyps load the lode   & awful hopeful at it.

...!!!] then I'm at last quiet.
        my daughter, black girl, rattles,
at me, her scabbard of tears.

my younger cousins, black women, their tears are:
- (A) pill bottles
- (B) in pill bottles
- (C) lids you press down, then turn to loose
- (D) anything bottled & near bathroom mirrors

likely my father's oldest sister, black woman,
kept her tears where they'd pass for shotgun:
     slant shade the jamb threw as simmering mask.

     my father's other sister, her tears stop his mouth,
or they're wood doves, cote'd in his chestnut mind?

grandmother, my black father's mother? gone.
her tears were empty chairs: pine
                    among pine-ware.

white bowl   though the rice there was tears of my great aunt,
black woman.

these days, my grandmother, black woman who mothered my mother,
mislays her tears—she always finds them in the,
                    finds them in,
                    finds them—.

the black woman who married me,
her tears inside her out like black church stockings / runs.

& my black mother dead.

Ecce Cuniculus

erewhay quod oleray autem Istchray autem ationsstay
autem osscray dun ayedplay per Erbray Abbitray.

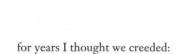

for years I thought we creeded:
was crucified under unconscious pilot.

thus, who flew this whole thing wasn't woke.
the stone rolled away and Christ, rock.

—D.K.

~~JESUS~~ [BRER RABBIT] IS CONDEMNED TO DEATH.
Pontius Pilate condemns ~~Jesus~~ [Brer Rabbit] to death.

Pilate a foxy red toga, rocks togs on some curtain for this here Theater of Suffering.

PP's olive pulp-plump palms all Palmolived®—raise your hem, Pees: show time!

in the spotlit spot where Jesu usu. bleeds: ecce—?

yellow pellet peat heap wreaks a fare-thee-well while Pontius and the Posture of Plausible Deniabilities!

on gog, CROWD beckons "ecce—? ecce—?"

Centurions (WOOT!) scourge; even the nothing they took for nothing from jump, the coney's shit orbs skitter the cruor cured stone like marbles at muhfuckas' mad aggie flogging.

madder light of broken day through selenium rubied spatters of stained glass mounts the show how we like and bright.

one soldier pricks himself *fuck* plucking briar to loop to a chaplet cap, crown for a king he'd whip-up.

you don't add no gold the red fades and fades.

~~JESUS~~ [BRER RABBIT], ~~TAKES UP HIS~~ CROSS.
~~Jesus willingly accepts and patiently bears his cross.~~

...relieved, but here to relieve: dere he go: hare, ọn sight on site now.

on some *oh hell no*...at the 8-stone x-axis of agony.

lippity.

scratching the flashing unstains stained glass thus staining its itness, Rabbit looses the rabbet with his nails, ...*hell I look like?*

clippitily he leaves the frame of being lit through for our relief.

the lone crossbeam, prone, minus sign and the difference.

anon to Via Dolorosa, the procession processes.

can't can't can't miss the praxis of transubstantiating gore to Cheer®!

~~JESUS~~ [BRER RABBIT] FALLS THE FIRST TIME.
~~Weakened by torments and by loss of blood,~~
~~Jesus~~ [Brer Rabbit] falls beneath ~~his cross.~~

I'm not where I'm flung at thus

under to the stuck cursive patch,

up down there, defoxed, 's'why out me a holler

flies, a jeer at a hunger,
other's. over origins
(the holler) and assorted conditions therein,
composed it was. for I declare,
I clarify most while I'm ghost.

viscous pitch, the burrs it picks-

up, so what kinda slick is it? I fix
to go down in dark thicket.
thorns crown my head,
brown and listening
for famished red. sunset,

fang-lit. lip-

pity clippity. tufts of where I was was about but where I
went wasn't.

thus, I am—[sic, y'all!]—

I 'is.'

~~JESUS~~ [BRER RABBIT] MEETS ~~HIS~~ SORROWFUL MOTHER.
~~Jesus~~ [Brer Rabbit] meets ~~His~~ mother, Mary, who is filled with grief.

avoiding enrobed hoi polloi 'pity 'pity pitters Rabbit.

Sup? says he, at knee-brake sundry.

^^ a means of inquiry.

He's not there were you there and the torments must go on mustn't they, for the tremble tremble tremble—thus walla sorrowers, the patibulum stalled on the thrashing room floor, the hraka canicas still in scattered lay.

shrugs at something, the sly judge.

meh, Brer finds the tribute pennies he finds find their way down his dungaree: lucky day!

but before drylongso woe pause his paws—the Mamamary pietà-nigh.

Ave, ma'am, why you weeping, why you mourning?

her tears nickeled glass on the ave.

why why why she cries, knowing.

eyes pried wide, she prays, groaning: *hhhhuh hhhhuh hhhhuh!*

etc. ecce itchy- /sticky-fingered Rabbit a shine took RE: the tears, pockets them on yoink.

they click a bit of ditty boinging up the Way of Hhhhuh.

SIMON OF CYRENE ~~HELPS JESUS~~ CARRY THE CROSS.
Soldiers force Simon of Cyrene to carry the cross.

flinching toward a lynching to gnash on, the mass was there when they—.

on cue debarks internash new booty fresh off the.

welcome welcome(!).

flare fissures when "guesting" his [conscripted] shoulder to the were you there when they—.

these ways is strange, says Simon of Cyrene.

Simon of Cyrene fixed to tote the beam.

welcome welcome(!) [GNASH].

Rabbit deep up the cut, about because folk need a thing to suffer.

[aside] "that timber won't carry itself, Simon of Cyrene.

"someone must do this labor."

[aside aside] "his trapezius does, boss."

"around here we pass the buck like a hot nigger killer—"

that last a way to say *red-skinned tater*. [GNASH]

these ways is strange, says Simon of Cyrene, beam to his back.

a flare a crack a krak.

he could (he *could*) get it, but this time, no (renounce abjure(¡!)): where there's spoor, there's hare there there's hare there's hope that to the hole's blackness *some* shit finds its way.

Simon may one day say this to his Children of Jerusalem, while larking, they take turns picking at that splinter ever interred in the Cyrenean's skin.

VERONICA ~~WIPES~~ THE FACE OF ~~JESUS~~.
Veronica steps through the crowd to wipe the face of ~~Jesus.~~

was she named she was for what she done; was what
she done named for who she was?

for the former they may saint her: cursive on a
corpse, sorta.

towel defurled, V(v)eronica, how long she sits very
quiet and still, as in calme.

as in some awe-mill's hallowed sun filter?

how long till oh tremble tremble tremble and the
big entrance — that LAT. *true image* a holy Polaroid®
she shake, there to bear the Xerox® of the One some
come to hiss to a mess of selenium-tint lightstain?

and if so, now that He ain't there but there he is in
His stead, unsteady understudy not studyin(g) this
Play, fleet bit of lip' clip' caper cutter, no woe-bough
weighed-down shoulder, no sweat to blot, no blood,
tears even, what's she to do if she's only what'll do;
her blank hanky wan, lank in fumblesome wind,
none's likeness pressed to re-member?

~~JESUS~~ [BRER RABBIT] FALLS A SECOND TIME.
~~Jesus~~ [Brer Rabbit] falls ~~beneath the weight of the cross~~
a second time.

I go down to be out,
being in's prey's ambition.

I jump because
to jump disses flight
since down's parcel to it—
not its fail.

every angel is terrible
at jumping. every angel's
partial, also.

I am a hole what lives
in a whole.

~~JESUS~~ [BRER RABBIT] MEETS THE WOMEN OF JERUSALEM.
~~Jesus~~ [Brer Rabbit] tells the women to weep not for him
but for themselves and for their children.

~~Jesus~~ [Brer Rabbit] tells the women to weep not for him
but for themselves ~~and for their children.~~

~~Jesus~~ [Brer Rabbit] tells the women to weep not for him
~~but for themselves and for their children.~~

~~Jesus~~ [Brer Rabbit] tells the women to weep not ~~for him~~
~~but for themselves and for their children.~~

knee-high to a crowd roused by the by-and-by snuff-show, the bunny eyefuls tented linens—uncuts and circumcisions less circumspect in tumescence, prime time such as it was/is.

making a way through, Brer makes it rain with the coins he came up on.

and surveying, Brer on swerve, curves over on some *yo mama* and *yo bébé*, Friday: the ladies on the Main Drag of Sad bearing itty itty fry swaddle—Function-going, prime time such as it was/is.

to the ladies in the front: tell 'im what you want:

another's (B)blood at issue?

another's (B)body to be, at last, barrow for a culture's dirt?

the blank station of INSERT HERE bends the corner, Simon in tow toting.

on some scuse me miss, Rabbit, knee-high: what's all the hubbub, bubbuleh?

: oh, they're going to kill Him!

: *him whom?*

: Him Him.

: *Him, him?*

: yes, Him!

: *naw, He ain't there and he's right here and not inclined to die for. so...*

but they woke up this A.M. with their minds set on Him, thus this Play, because!

weeping, that nickeled way wet for the Big Finish what begins us all (-1) anew and clean, yes—

fuck it, full up of foreground ruckus, Rabbit cuts out the queue, ducks a monger hustling mutton on the middle plane for where shadow thickets leadfully.

~~JESUS~~ [BRER RABBIT] FALLS THE THIRD TIME.
~~Weakened almost to the point of death, Jesus~~
[Brer Rabbit] falls a third time.

was there a hole in His Hand
I'd dive in and He would go in after me
and out the other side
and I'd go back in His palm and He'd
dive into Himself and out
as I'm in again and He

and I'd be the hell out and in

He'd be in then out as He

got the hang of it and roll away,

turning in the circle that's Himself

of Himself. amen.

~~JESUS IS~~ STRIPPED ~~OF HIS~~ GARMENTS.
The soldiers strip ~~Jesus of his~~ garments, ~~treating him~~
~~as a common criminal.~~

abracadabra!

rags once clothes, lickety-split aloft then somer-slump to the dust, piling textile nimbus for (H)he who wasn't there.

and more garment swatches arc to drop, flip flopping motley into laundry mounds that crowd the Centurions (woot!) hawking spit at what kit they don't hock dear.

(there's a kind what buys a tooth booted out a jaw to gawk at, nails the hank of uprooted hair to have, to apprehend what's apprehended—their hearts, windowless black vans).

past that tatter shower, Brer Rabbit secrets taproot from retail stalls.

marinate on this ironical food.

what's pulled from dirt can keep you out of it.

how he savors subterranean!

> *o little root of nourishment*
> *how crunchy to my mouth!*
> *above my tongue and past my gums*
> *to pellets out my south.*

rough harvest, the flung garments—there they go to scape.

V(v)eronica's taut limb tremble tremble trembling, Simon leaning on the beam to someone's summer idyll, and Pees parts the red seam it all seeps out, bleeding over the kingless soldier suckling blood from his stuck opposable.

at the stall, Brer deposits the stained nickel scrap he pocketed, moved thus.

straight up, the stipes was there pining for the cross beam was there for the nails and the Body that wasn't there nor the body.

the crowd was there for the Blood that wasn't nor the blood.

the stipes tight in its hole.

the Centurions (woot!) tally bones' pips, jab javelins at air, spit a spit up gravity spits back down, their sour grimaces a-froth with viscous cloud clod.

the crowd, interpellatish at this x-marked [...], thirsty as double-mouthed cups with their thirst.

hungry with their hunger as double-mouthed bowls, but calling on and on for the Blood or some blood and the soldiers, despondent, spittled white, probe the Tree for fruit, spears mere loppers.

ecce reapers-of-representative-suffering unsuffered, a forfeited surfeit of puppetted letting, a throng of groan ventriloquists, put out with what work it takes to put in work.

(the tar babe was never no Lester, no Lambchop, but a way to stuck you there.)

a detail among stalls—free-browsing, bean-feasting —Brer Rabbit casts a _{him} of himself with himself—his fist, the middle, the index, his shade thrown haintly in the market's fading mid-day patina.

"were you there when they crucified my Lord?"

a spiritual of known unknowns, call to LARP (as are all rituals), the participants (SINGER and LISTENER[1]) seek to embody the THEM-THEN[2] while remaining THEM-NOW; thus not the THEM-THEN.

yet, as a vehicle in an (a)synchronous, religious ritual, the instrumentally embodied singer (SINGER or LISTENERS who (A) *mutually affirms* or (B) *confirms* the inquiry) must not *perform* THEM-THEN's feelings, but *have* THEM-THEN's feelings while singing now.

when in singing, SINGER opens its mouth to ask "were you there when they crucified my Lord?"

this question signals the song's liturgical purpose: LISTENERS must be THEM-THEN, as LISTENERS are the "you" (THEM-THEN) the lyrics call.

yet LISTENERS are also of course THEMSELVES-NOW.[3]

the call (as a *rhetorical question* or *question*) provides a vehicle for participants'[4] embodiment of THEM-THEN; not THEMSELVES-AS-THEM-THEN, rather as the THEM-NOW themselving themselves to those who were THEM-THEN (witnesses of the Crucifixion).

---

[1] the LISTENER subjectivity may include SINGER (sometimes SINGER sings both question ["were you there..."] and reply ["sometimes it causes me to tremble! tremble! tremble!"]), other SINGERS [antiphony], and the congregation/audience. God, Whom the song glorifies, is LISTENER, not LISTENERS.

[2] those that were actually "there when they crucified my Lord."

[3] which, at the time of this writing, follows the event by about 2,000 years.

[4] *participants* indicates SINGER and LISTENER en masse.

participants become THEMSELVES-NOW-THEM-THEN.

ipso facto: the lyrics identify (primarily) two witness types—(A) THEM-THENS who were *there-when*[5] "they crucified my Lord" and (B) THEM-THENS who were there-*when*[6] "they crucified my Lord."

the question: "were you there when they crucified my Lord?" hails both witness-types through (A) *mutual affirmation* or (B) *confirmation*, respectively.

(A) *mutual affirmation*: SINGER witnessed the event and asks if LISTENERS were (<u>also</u>) *there-when*; thus SINGER-itself-singing must have seen what LISTENERS as THEMSELVES-NOW-THEM-THEN saw.

SINGER, via a rhetorical version of the question, asks what it knows already: that the LISTENER was *there-when* because SINGER, too, was *there-when*.

SINGER stakes affirmation of the embodiment on *the event itself*, a metonymic transubstantiation proposing a collective subjectivity of THEMSELVES-NOW-THEM-THEN (SINGER singing now of only what THEM-THEN could—but LISTENERS *must*—know), leaping temporal and geographic distance between now and the event—*there* and *when* are operative: SINGER *and* LISTENERS are *there-when* and *here-now*.

(B) *confirmation*:[7] an entreaty of LISTENERS for the LISTENERS' news of the event.

---

5   thus geographically *and* temporally.

6   thus only temporally.

7   LISTENERS were there when they crucified my Lord, but SINGER was not.

here, SINGER's distance from the event is geographic and temporal (*there-when*); operatively, the question is temporal (SINGER *must* sing now of then [*when*]; the site [*there*] is ostensibly available)—the inquiry is no longer particularly about proximity, but time.[8]

it is also no longer rhetorical.

SINGER is, here, *itself*, thus someone who did not witness the event, and must ask THEM-THEN by way of LISTENERS as THEMSELVES-NOW-THEM-THEN.

instrumentally, LISTENERS are in place to confirm what SINGER has taken on—thus, proposes as—faith.

in neither case is the question generally one of skepticism (SINGER's at the prospect of the event ["were you there when they 'crucified' my Lord?" or LISTENERS' presence there ["were *you* there when they crucified my Lord?"]); though *trembling*'s ambiguity (sorrow? rage? passion? fatigue?) could describe a response to a crisis of faith.

such doubt would disrupt the participants' passage to THEMSELVES-NOW-THEM-THEN (those themselves who *could* bear witness and *must* for the ritual at hand); if no participant could bear witness, there is no *there-when* to see, and as such, no Crucifixion.

but here, He isn't here, nor is the hare there; still something "needs" suffering...

8   essential to the spiritual's functionality is *when*. the temporal potential to have witnessed the Crucifixion is paramount to SINGER's inquiry which becomes the vehicle for LISTENERS' embodiment of THEM-THEN as THEMSELVES-NOW-THEM-THEN.

~~JESUS IS TAKEN DOWN~~ FROM THE CROSS.
~~The lifeless body of Jesus~~ [Brer Rabbit] is tenderly placed
in the arms of Mary, ~~his mother.~~

~~The lifeless body of Jesus~~ [Brer Rabbit] ~~is tenderly placed
in the arms of~~ Mary, ~~his mother.~~

might thaw cockle to re-recast Rabbit as a service
pet Mamamary petted, a pietà cottontail to curtail
her wailing; but Brer won't serve.

capers cut, sated by way of fugitivity, he's slipping
off home again, home again lippity clip.

the assembled seek a vessel for their mess.

so of Mamamary, ringed by throng on hushing,
make a bowl of her bowed arms, of her lap make a
cup, her composed dolor.

curved, again, round a will not hers, Mamamary's
pose poses a lippity clippity pity: *there now there
there isn't [...] there now?*

but when it isn't, what is?

when it won't, what will?

what might we mold to void the void that voids
the pietà, decomposes Mamamary to the rest of us
poised to pose in possession of what we lost?

to sob for its death to clot our sobbing?

to ache for its death to balm our aching?

to feel it as we feel it must have felt it, mustn't it, just for us?

to rise from its death, the moment of the passing passing, as if passing by the other sad passersby down the Sad Passage, passing past; till it passes that we pass a platter at the repast, and what's passed for us passes over the same tearing teeth we'll bare for smiling when this passes and draw when we'll surely want more—forks' hands bearing what died for us to the tombs our mouths turned.

~~JESUS~~ [BRER RABBIT] IS ~~LAID~~ IN ~~THE TOMB.~~
~~Jesus' disciples~~ place his body in ~~the tomb~~.

yonder in skull hill's hole, Brer Rabbit, belly-filled,
slumbers like a window with no sun through.

as such, he hutches his color his—the red in, the
brown on—nil spills to lend blood nor skin to those
prayers praying for Proxy, praying for He who in
skulls-set-on-Him may lay.

the melee, resetful, makes for the city's thresholds.

trembling trembling trembling, the wan hanky, at
last, drops.

a fox-colored judge scrubs and scrubs another's
blood: a way to say, "I wasn't there."

were you?

blanched cloth alights on the dark earth, looks a
bass-ackward hole.

tears mistify into a spittle what could grow things
though.

spears remember they're step-kin to fingers, hunger
again to touch someone.

fertile shit marbles husk away, wasted on cobble.

No Wake/Too Much of Fucking Everything

after Robert Rauschenberg's Short Stories

"Too much of fucking everything..."

—N.M.

The following poems document time spent at
the Rauschenberg Residency on Captiva Island,
Florida—mostly in July 2014.

Children were present.

"be certain nothing's living in that shell."

NO TRESPASSING

STRANGLER FIG GREAT FOR BIRDS!

lizards strip tree litter
pell-skeltering the jungle road,
palm over, and moringa,
those palmettos we can't see won't skitter
till night bruises the kitchens.

too much of fucking everything.

SUBJECT TO FINE!

NO TRESPASSING

Edgar swore he saw
the milky way,
a manatee glowing
in the shallow, bay
dark—beautiful magical,
then off he's to scrape at vanities.
project: a vandalized cathedral,
stained stained glass.
a shame.

kills the palmettos waterbugs cockroaches on contact!

THE HOUSES
AND THE BOATS
HAVE NAMES
HERE! PARADISE
PARADISE
PARA...

NO TRESPASSING

your heart.

"you want to look inside
the suicide letter,
a space age dream today
"I Have A Dream." toady
say it's not easy.

in the cinderblock
compost bunker
tomorrow molders.
vermin aren't mean,
but hungry.

It's a discipline to keep
your door unlocked.

NO TRESPASSING

they peck and peck
the fruit of murder.

"I'll just throw it back in.
because it smells."

AT #2 RAISE THE MOTOR OUT AND GUN IT
up the shins SET FOR 40° IN REVERSE 15–20 SECONDS
in adventure. CUTS THE WEEDS.

I can see the lizard's bones!
I can see the lizard's bones!

past the hurricane glass stalks calico parabola
wending the wicker chairs on jook status,
bat-eared and boon-ful, altogether longer
than the housecat I took it for,
the shoulder taller than my knee.
bobcat's in high cotton of marsh bunnies,
a springing spring rebounds
from Charlie's once wet leveling.

IDLE SPEED NO WAKE

RESUME NORMAL SAFE OPERATION

well maybe a bird, honey.
or maybe he just got old, honey.
with all these bugs,
he wasn't hungry!
see? the skin's like paper.
that's where his eyes were, dear.

it had really done a number!

all this rain's
why the air
bites me.

Fred asked whether the place looked different.

but I don't want to see the lizard!

one of the girls was stung.

:01
:02
:03
:04
:05
:06
:07
:08
:09
:10
:11
:12
:13
:14
:15
:16
:17
:18
:19
:20

sound smashed-and-grabbed
the archipelago, spoils
in the cabbage soup tide's out.
if you want to get home heave-
the pontoon boat
de-hill to the sludge I stuck us
-ho sputter down near petering
to deeper shallows.
trudged scallop shells shard out glass
and snot, in the furtive brackish rushes.

ENTER:
THE STRANGERS
OF KINDNESS

un-agrounded off
my bad.

the other artists quit their work
to see a steamroller happening
to Kate's cubic metal sculpture.
at last the crushed structure
by Bobcat reverse and brake
and drive till the secreted sac
bursts and red paint!

blackflytips
hammerheads—no,
masonry plated hornets
drill and trowell
the muddy knuckle duster
throbbing in the crux
of the clapboard eave.

THE MAN OVERBOARD PIZZA IS TOPPED WITH
PEPPERONI SAUSAGE GREEN PEPPERS, BLACK
OLIVES, fucking everything MROOMS.
too much of

CAPTIVA CELEBRATION PLAZA
ONLY

GET A SLICE OF ISLAND LIFE!

ice cubes for ruddy
boils, she reacts to
bug bites, goes   bog-wash and shlopping mud
writhing and   cede to waxy grass,
larval, transverse,   a green that heebie jeebies.
to his lap, body   pale crabs guerilla there
unclotted and   gnats ack-ack the magic hour.
sudden at it,   Theraflu air cools and *sky's like*
table cloth up   *sherbet* says Anselm rainbows and
checked, livid,   rainbows! rubbled exoskeletal
then pallid,   hulls jag, snaking ways past the
livid, pallid,   fish house.
livid in
the slow   NO TRESPASSING
eatery.   Carell says, *it's going to be bloody.*
              so kids peel from the sly bayside pod,
              watch the blade find critical red:
              concealed slice behind snapper gill,
              triple-time ticking muscle,
              —like a lizard's tail.
              first you clean the fish.
              then you gut the fish.

that long.
but the effects don't last
it got my hand he said.
hurt for about 20 minutes he said.

NO BEACH PARKING

wading, you shuffle.
graceful shy creatures
in sand are painful,
but it's just a nature.

past the sea grass lashes, up the gradual dune-rise,
slouches the beach house. like ants on a red vine
the sand on our legs and millipede panzers
storm the shower's concrete slab. children
worry for their feet, they screech and tear
at the dampening, teeming ground.

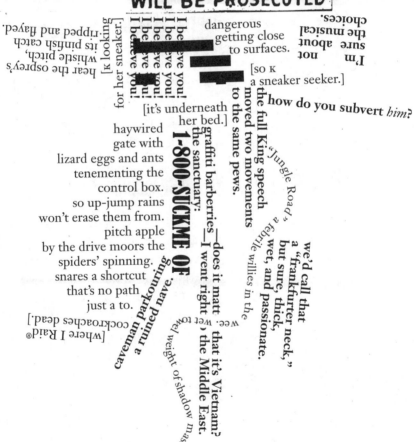

TRESPASSERS
WILL BE PROSECUTED

ripped and flayed.
its pinfish catch
whistle pitch,
hear the osprey's

for her sneaker.]

[K looking

I believe you!
I believe you!
I believe you!
I believe you!
I believe you!
I believe you!

dangerous
getting close
to surfaces.

I'm not sure about the musical choices.

[so K a sneaker seeker.]

[it's underneath her bed.]

to the same pews.
moved two movements
the full King speech

how do you subvert *him?*

haywired
gate with
lizard eggs and ants
tenementing the
control box.
so up-jump rains
won't erase them from.
pitch apple
by the drive moors the
spiders' spinning.
snares a shortcut
that's no path
just a to.

1-800-SUCKME OF

the sanctuary:
graffiti barberries—
—I went right
does it matt   that it's Vietnam?
) the Middle East.

"Jungle Road", a febrile willies in the

we'd call that
a "frankfurter neck,"
but sure, thick,
wet, and passionate.

[where I Raid® cockroaches dead.]

caveman parkouring
a ruined nave.

wee. wet towel
weight of shadow mass.

Matt says:
"cut clean through
the meat to her titanium
implant broke the prop!"
everyone's all 'what stars chop in on those helicopters' the waitress says.

there are sharks where?
EVERYBODY COME INSIDE!

"IF YOU'RE IMPATIENT,
YOU'RE IN THE WRONG
PLACE. "always carry Tampax!"

downy clouds boll
the island over,
bogarting how blue it
was, forking lightning for
to lit the green-smacked
canopy and reboot. CLOUD-
TO-GROUND

*the choppers
are airlifting traumas
to hospitals.*

fire across the sound
piles a billow-boil
behind the artists.
it's controlled. SMILE!

EVERYBODY COME INSIDE!

oh. [deflate]
*well here go
your shrimp!*

MKT. PRICE

shock and eat
shuck and awe
scrumptious!

sssssssssssssssssssssss
sssssssssssssssssss
ssssssssssss
sssssss
sss

"I said, 'buy a lottery ticket…!'"
where
the airlift field
and come to
biting dusk,
white ibis
haintpacks on
some Wild
Hunt strike—
all bobbing red
scythes—
plucking cock-
roaches from
St. Augustine
bosk. oh the
pretty oh how
pretty birds.

83

"a kind of handcuffs,"
Karen explains.
SU–TH 8:00–6:00

no moan black snake up
to ratting (radial rubber
shred long and rearing),
to tangle in the root-
work, the interdigitated,
trunks' frondled cavern
of bark callous
and dew. it
get in there and
gone.

*too much of fucking
everything*

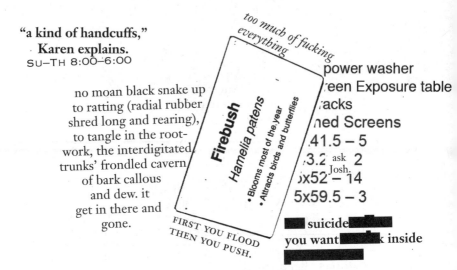

Firebush
Hamelia patens
• Blooms most of the year
• Attracts birds and butterflies

FIRST YOU FLOOD
THEN YOU PUSH.

power washer
:een Exposure table
·acks
ned Screens
.41.5 – 5
.3.2 ask 2
Josh.
)x52 – 14
5x59.5 – 3

suicide
you want   k inside

the closest we'll ever come to having sex.

PRIVATE ROAD.
NO UNAUTHORIZED
VEHICLES
the gulf licks and licks,
coquina and cockles
dig slick into the silt.

"I RECOMMEND
FIFTY SHADES OF GRAY."

horny red figments
pigment mark a silhouette—
nipples: bright mosquito bites,
pubic hair: brush fire on pine island,
abdomen: rat snake down to ratting.

FLOOD
PUSH
FLOOD
PUSH
FLOOD
PUSH
FLOOD
PUSH

I'd just bleed all over you.

FR–SA 8:00–8:00

"...lives in a world
full of wonder..."

pojoe from *poor joe*
from the legs
like starving,
thrift weft
of the plumage,
lank-slung neck
gawp gawp gawp
sloshes the heron
in reed-studded
stuporous
summer bug fog,
mullet upflung
from their turvy
dis-earth.

to break the sound —
clamor for a sign of pescatarian dildos
rut tide.
a four-pod
then: green waters.

so pojoe goes
on ding darling's gawk-ready
plankway,
on the splintery rail of the
stilty fish house, spindly gojira
to them poets' fam-bam:
an awed American city along

first glimpse of the heron, I penned "basilisk."

"Tricks ~~he~~ she will do
when children appear"

"No-one you see,
is smarter than ~~he~~ she."

THE MALES SCARRED [marred]
FROM FIGHTING [martial]
SO THE FEMALES GIVE BETTER
CAMERA [marvie]

CLAP!
SHOUT!
THEY'LL PUT ON
A SHOW FOR US!

THEY LOVE
OUR NOISE!

all the dim dolphin thumb
my all the lens angled.

in this time
this time
this time
I make a promise of it.
next time
next time
next time
I fake an answer out it.

Anselm!!!   *Anselm!!!!*
            Anselm!!!!
      Anselm!!!!

I holler from the craft
since so pressed to name
what I know= a hardening
on the sound.

WATCH YOUR STEP:
TALL LIP!

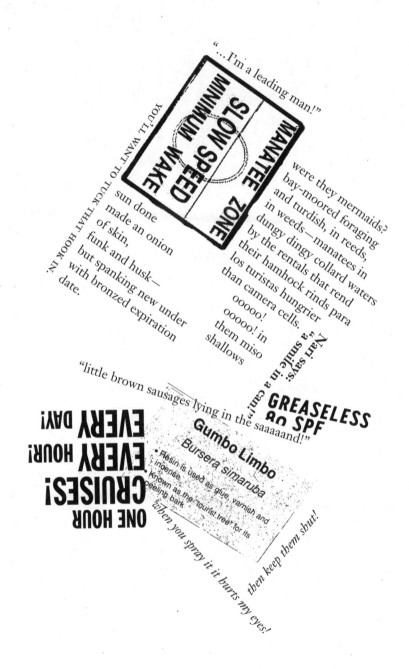

" ...I'm a leading man!"

MANATEE ZONE
MINIMUM
SLOW SPEED
WAKE

YOU'LL WANT TO TUCK THAT HOOK IN;

sun done
made an onion
of skin,
funk and husk—
but spanking new under
with bronzed expiration
date.

were they mermaids?
bay-moored foraging
and turdish, in reeds,
in weeds—manatees in
dungy dingy collard waters
by the rentals that rend
their hamhock rinds para
los turistas hungrier
than camera cells.
ooooo!
ooooo! in
them miso
shallows

Nari says: "a smile in a can

GREASELESS
OR SPF

"little brown sausages lying in the saaaaand!"

Gumbo Limbo
Bursera simaruba

• Resin is used as glue, varnish and
  incense.
• Known as the "tourist tree" for its
  peeling bark

EVERY DAY!
EVERY HOUR!
CRUISES!
ONE HOUR

when you spray it it burns my eyes!

then keep them shut!

Kate recalls "they got dizzy
staring at all that pink
for tens of minutes."

STRICTLY
ENFORCED

loggerheads set to a magnetic
shore a score and nickel since
slipping the cormorant shivs and
bulleting gull bills off the gulf sill.
awww soft hull totterings exodus
the pail, desperate ripples in tidal
shelter. the shells have backbone
and hard odds. clawed fiddlers
for dishes best served cold, mama
logger need some
vindication
for the clutch.

"shattered ceramics—
I was gravid,
perhaps I shouldn't have
laddered..."
the big girls did just fine,
the skinny ones kept fainting.

*I think the ones with wings
are boys and don't bite, sting,
anything*

pink pink pink
pink pink pink
pink pink pink
ink pink pink pink pink
ink pink pink pink pink
ink pink pink pink
ink pink pink

COULD BREAK YOUR ARM.
THEIR JAWS
WE'RE VOLUNTEERS

all that pink
pink pink pink
pink pink
pink pink pink
pink pink pink
pink pink pink
pink pink
pink pink

we'll release them after dusk

they were all paid.

NO FLASHES, PLEASE!
NO FLASHES, PLEASE!
NO FLASHES, PLEASE!

SUBJECT
TO FINE!

*yes, hon, just like the cartoon,
we can't touch them.
no, they need the ocean.*

"better than Queenie"
no one does it
to this cool treat,
"When it comes"

NO LIGHTS. THE HATCHLINGS
GET DISORIENTED.

THE QUEEN OF ICE CREAM

Terri brought soup!
pink pink pink pink pink pink
pink pink pink pink pink

just [plop.]

well, they could die.

the one with the hottest bod
and everyone knows it.

low, sun's an oleo pat
on strawberry flapjack batter
run into third coast broth.

and pink and
pink and pink
and pink and
pink and pink
and pink
*everything
too much of fucking*

SUBJECT
TO FINE!

IT'S NATURE'S
WAY, THE
GULLS—
just...

our kids' eat.
about how we feed

TRESPASSERS
WILL BE PROSECUTED

of a sudden flood come sudden
flood up ruddy ducts of mud
puncta and out they a wind of
wound and wounding the grounds,
fronds, grit, the shell shard wend-
way slick asheen, tabasco fanged
damasked march, tibial spurs as a
NO YOU trillion shanks, red ruckle, ruckus
HAVE A brung, hungry trickle, stinging milk
PROBLEM. back in the muck nipple nest.

OK! OK! CALM DOWN!

"A 'Mobile' Market from Matlacha"

GET A SLICE
OF ISLAND LIFE!

OUTSIDE
THE DINING ROOM
SLIDING DOOR
the microgecko carcass
a bindle of pinky parings.
the microgecko carcass
a nori swatch of slivers.
the microgecko carcass
a sachet of filthy thread.
the microgecko carcass
a beedi of blonde clippings.

I AM CALM!

"Special Orders & Delivery"

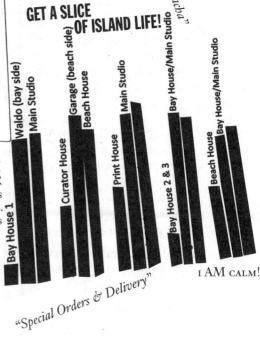

Australian Pine
Casuarina quisetifolia
Topples easily in storms
Competes with native species

Bay House 1
Waldo (bay side)
Main Studio
Curator House
Garage (beach side)
Beach House
Print House
Main Studio
Bay House 2 & 3
Bay House/Main Studio
Beach House
Bay House/Main Studio
Bay House

Headnote to a Done Poem

for Wanda Coleman

Dear L.A.,
I am sorry for your—Dear

Baja and Bay, I am sorry
for your—Dear Jagged West,
I am sorry for

your—Dear Aged East,
I am sorry for your—Dear Shine

to Seas, I am sorry for

your—Dear Pole to Pole, I am
sorry for your—Dear Ice
and Soil, I am sorry

for your—Dear Ear Canaled, I

am sorry for your—Dear Eyeballed,
I am sorry for your—Dear Tongued

and Dear Thumbed, I am

sorry for your—Dear Nostrilled,
oh my dear Nostrilled, I am sorry for your loss,
your loss of the funk, your funkless,
bereft loss of that gut bucket busting
with Birds of Paradise, church socks,
with coffee grounds and soggy paperbacks.

whiffs of ziplocked poppies and pissways,
boocoo tail pipes belting yellow notes and backfire.
ramschackled passels of green apples under underpasses.
oil paints gone fungal under summer sun.
of kerosene, the rainbow in the Valvoline pool
and the bronzed coin slicked gold down there.

Dear South L.A.,
I am sorry for your loss of Central,
ghost now, ganked and gaffled,
cuffed and trunked with stuff we knew
and stuff we don't, stuff we was meant to get,
to hold to, but butterfingered, let slip.
stuff we figured we'd catch next time round,
but it was Sunday at midnight at a bus stop, Watts—
and the street gone dark for going mute.

Dear Salt Petered 110,
Dear Weird Skied 10,
Dear Mortared 405,
Dear Spider Legged 5,
Dear Wheezing 14,
I regret your riverboat queenlessness,
the white-walled paddlewheel moored in the dock.
gnash and chomp over this new dry-spell,
holler for your tarred beds and stiff necks.

Dear Soap Operas and Soapboxes,
I am sorry for your— Dear
Chitins and Chitlins, I am sorry for
your—Dear Pink Slips and Slipper Print,
I am sorry for your—

Dear Civic Offices of Wrung Hands and Ringing Lines,
I regret to be informed of this new Earthquake cure.
that our smogscrapers won't come to shiver
with pleasure, with terror, with snits.
I regret the asphalt won't fault to black cracks
jabbing down to Earth's orange heart,
Dear Crust, Dear Mantle. sorry no bell will
toll us below our tables. Dear Formica,
Dear Veneer, I'm sorry we won't peer
beneath you and find hard fists of Bubblicious.

Dear Mouthful of Oysters and Seeds, I am
sorry for your—Dear Mouthful of Pop Bottles,
I am sorry for your—Dear Mouthful
of 45s and Candy Hearts,
I regret you must peck bread at a stranger's park bench,
peck bread out a new bag, sweet flock. a new pocket, hot damn.

Dear Throat of Grout, Throat of Fruit,
I regret the loss of low down loupsgarou,
of toe-holed nylon. a bushel of neon onions on a Zenith,
unpeeling. the peal of sand pelting corrugated steel, stolen.
the quiet storm that slumbers behind molars, pulled.
the daybreak bitten like a kumquat, puked.
the slow drag's sloe wound, the rag's ragged, sink-bound flight.
the alley's gold teeth. the floor fan's hum as it rumbles with July.

Dear Amnesiac Eardrums,
I am—forget it.
Dear Channel Surfing No-see-ums,
I am—never mind.
Dear Ruffled Hatchlings,
I am sorry for your pinions, your guano tinted lenses,
for your shook-assery at tremors, and your tattooed blacklists,
your little yellow tongues. I am sorry for big feet,
the Blue Parade, turned Blue Cortege, turned Second Line,
all the pages it left, all the papers that pile
your boulevard cobbled with eggshells.
Dear Armless Palm Trees,

I am sorry you could not catch her,
Dear Armless Palm Trees,

why couldn't you catch her?

Dear Children of the, of the—,
my great regret for reckoning you wouldn't want,
all what's left below folding chairs,
in garage-rotting boxes,
and by the final curb,
her words where her picture would be,
the picture where her words.

Dear What's Left of Us,
I regret we didn't know
a mind like a heart
was no mark-ass simile.
Dear Family
Dear Austin
Dear

I

Notes and Acknowledgments

STAGGER PUT WORK IN

Stagolee Shot Billy by Cecil Brown, *Stagger Lee* by Derek McCulloch and Shepherd Hendrix, the *Bibliotheca* by Diodorus Siculus, and www.perseus.tufts.edu/ Herakles/ labors.html were of great help in researching these poems.

"Mane" quotes Lloyd Price/Harold Logan's "Stagger Lee." It also riffs off "Whatta Man" by Salt N Pepa/EnVogue, and dialogue from Eddie Murphy's *The Nutty Professor*.

"Necks" quotes a blues version of "Stagger Lee" performed by John Cephas and Phil Wiggins. This happens again in "Trim" and "Mouth Mouth Mouth."

"Shot" quotes Price/Logan's "Stagger Lee." In "The Gender of Sound," Anne Carson writes of *ololyga*:
> ...a particular kind of shriek, the ololyga. This is a
> ritual shout peculiar to females. It is a highpitched
> piercing cry uttered at certain climactic moments in
> ritual practice (e.g. at the moment when a victim's
> throat is slashed during sacrifice).

Also, transcribed in "Shot" is a standard G-Funk rhythm, variations of which appear elsewhere in the collection.

"Rooter" quotes The Coaster's "I'm a Hog" and alludes to a version of "Stagger Lee" sung by Nick Cave and the Bad Seeds.

"Shit" riffs on a few things—Maxwell's cover of a Kate Bush song, a Rita Dove poem, and there's Price/Logan again.

"Chrrrp" cribs its title from a poem in LaTasha N. Nevada Diggs' *TwERK*. It also nudges the pop hit, "Rockin' Robin" written by Leon René as Jimmie Thomas. However, I'm thinking of the Bobby Day version.

"Bully" interpolates a joke I first heard in the movie *Colors* as well as lyrics from "The Bully of the Town" (which seems to be "traditional") and "Boom Biddy Bye Bye" by Cypress Hill. Belluthahatchie and Diddy Wah Diddy are suburbs of Hell.

"Trim" riffs on lyrics from Willie Dixon's "Wang Dang Doodle," Snoop Doggy Dogg and Tha Dogg Pound's "Ain't No Fun (If the Homies Cant Have None)," Robert and Richard Poindexter's/Jackie Members' "It's a Thin Line (Between Love and Hate)," Mobb Deep's "Shook Ones, Pt. II," and Prince's "Strange Relationship." A *porte-jarretelles* is a garter belt. The asshole print comes from a version of "Stackolee" I read in Roger D. Abraham's *Afro-American Folktales*.

"Herd" owes content to the Cecil Brown observation that Bobby Seale would use versions of the Stagger Lee toast when recruiting for the Black Panthers. A supercell is a meteorological system.

"Mouth Mouth Mouth" quotes "Sexual Healing" by Marvin Gaye and "Stack O' Lee Blues" by Ma Rainey.

THAT LOUD-ASSED COLORED SILENCE

"That Loud-Assed Colored Silence: Booming System aka Miranda Rizights": *clap* can be slang for a gunshot.

"That Loud-Assed Colored Silence: Scat" quotes Mista Grim's "Indo Smoke," Eazy E's "Boyz-N-The-Hood," and The Roots' "The Next Movement."

"That Loud-Assed Colored Silence: Beat Music" misquotes Yusef Komunyakaa's "Ode to the Drum."

"Afrofuturism" reflects conversations I had with the late artist Terry Adkins and the artists Mike Demps and Lauren Halsey. It quotes "Inner City Blues" by Marvin Gaye, "Space is the Place" by Sun Ra, "The Middle Passage" by Robert Hayden, "Sea Cruise" (lyrics by Huey "Piano" Ford), and Soundwave from the 1980's animated series, *The Transformers*. It riffs off Janelle Monáe's "Q.U.E.E.N." and The Clipse's "Ride Around Shinin'."

"~~Kafk(-rik)a(n) (Merkin) Bop~~ AKA Woke Up This
Mornin' AKA da Mystery…" is a Bop, a form Afaa
Michael Weaver invented. Its refrain quotes
Raekwon's verse from "Da Mystery of Chessboxin'" by
The Wu-Tang Clan. It also quotes "Feeling Good" as
sung by Nina Simone, written by Anthony Newley/
Leslie Bricusse. I'd guess "Woke up this morning" is
a floating line from any number of Blues songs, but
I was thinking of Robert Johnson's "Preachin Blues."
Accidentally, Ol' Dirty Bastard closes.

"That Loud-Assed Colored Silence: Moan" chops
Run-DMC's "Peter Piper."

"That Loud-Assed Colored Silence: Protest" features
lyrics from a concert piece titled "Overcome" (a flip of
"We Shall Overcome"), written for Michael Skloff.

"Pornegrophy" quotes the traditional tune, "Train
Is A Comin'." "Love has nothing to do with it; love
has everything to do with it," is a quote from Saidiyah
Hartman's *Lose Your Mother: A Journey Along the Atlantic
Slave Route.*

THE BLACK WOMAN'S TEAR MONGER

"The Black Woman's Tear Monger" was influenced
in the main by Raymond Patterson's "26 Ways of
Looking at a Blackman."

"Big Thicket: Pastoral" is a response to the murder
of James Byrd, Jr. in Jasper, TX. Members of a White
Supremacist gang dragged him behind a pick-up truck
over several miles of Huff Creek Road along an area of
woodland called the Big Thicket.

"Niggas Be Watching the News in 2015, Y'all" is
written after Eileen Myles' "The Snakes."

"Lives" is for E, who was playing *Diversion* and *Fireman
Extreme*. A *shadow fade* is a style of haircut.

ECCE CUNICULUS

Ecce is Latin for "behold," as in *ecce homo*.

I sought out the source for the unmodified titles of these poems but could find no originary author.

Throughout the poems, there are a number of references to stained glass making and coloring. Artisans add selenium, for example, to produce red glass. Stained glass making terms include: *rabbet*, *calme*, and *flare*. Additionally, lyrics from the hymn "Were You There?" appear throughout.

Lippity Clippity, also used throughout, is taken from a Walt Disney publication of *Uncle Remus Stories*. It seems to mean "quickly" and "carefree."

Walla is a word film and TV extras repeat to simulate conversations in the background of scenes. *Hraka* is Lapine for "droppings, excreta" (Richard Adams).

Patibulum denotes the horizontal beam on a cross. The account I read stated they weighed 8-stone (112 LBS).

Stipes denotes the vertical post of a cross. Lester and Lambchop are famous puppets.

Resetful is not a typo. Neither is *mistify*.

NO WAKE/TOO MUCH OF FUCKING EVERYTHING

You can see pages from Robert Rauschenberg's *Short Stories* series at www.rauschenbergfoundation.org.

These poems feature appearances from my fellow residents, members of the Rauschenberg Foundation staff, the folks of Captiva, and Fred S. (by phone).

I quote the FBI on page 89. I quote the theme song to *Flipper* on page 95. I quote Tom Waits's "Going Out West" on page 96.

ACKNOWLEDGMENTS

Thank you to the editors who published versions of these poems in anthologies and journals.

JOURNALS

Alaska Quarterly Review, Bath House Review, Bengal Lights, Boston Review, Boundary 2, Brooklyn Rail, Catch Up, Círculo de Poesía, The Economy, Explosion Proof, Indiana Review, Lana Turner, LitHub, Poetry, Poets.org, Public Pool, Tidal Basin Review, Tripwire, Virginia Quarterly Review, The Volta

ANTHOLOGIES

Break Beat Poets: New American Poetry in the Age of Hip-Hop, Enclave: Poéticas Experimentales, Futurepoem's *Black Moon Tarot, Resisting Arrest: Poems to Stretch the Sky, The Ringing Ear: Black Poets Lean South*

"Drop It Like It's Hottentot Venus." and "Well Hung" appear in *SkinMag*, a chapbook published by A5/ Deadly Chaps (2012).

Several of the poems from the That Loud-Assed Colored Silence section are part of an oratorio, *The Freedom of Shadow*, composed in response to Terry Adkins and his work, sponsored by The Poetry Foundation and The Joan Mitchell Foundation.

...

There are many folks I'd like to thank in particular, though I am blessed with an abundance of supportive family, friends, colleagues, teachers, and readers.

To the Robert Rauschenberg Foundation for its tremendous support. I thank, foremost, the staff of the Rauschenberg Residency as led by Ann Brady; and to my fellow residents for generosity and rich conversations.

To my Aunt Dee, for always reading every word anyway.

To Jericho Brown, LaTasha N. Nevada Diggs, and Evie Shockley for reading and challenging early (and, E.S., 11ᵀᴴ-hour!) drafts of several of these poems. The value of your suggestions, provocations, and intelligence is rivalled only by that of your friendship.

Yona Harvey and Amaud Jamaul Johnson: I've walked with you since HU. There are no finer companions. Thank you for your generous early readings, good sense, and for all you continue to teach me.

To Tisa Bryant for patiently listening to me blather on about Brer Rabbit, sacrifice, and suffering; Anthony McCann, for your enthusiasm about the No Wake sequence; and to Wave Books + Machine Project for hosting and recording a reading of a version of this book.

To Miré Regulus who deserves my thanks for slanting me after G.E. Patterson's workshop on Strangeness way back in MPLS.

To the activists who work in hopes of keeping the execution of Black people in the streets from turning into white noise.

To Kwesi for the stuffed rabbit.

To The Black Took Collective, Ruth Ellen Kocher, and AJJ for those dope-ass drum rolls.

To Pops for singing all that music with me. To Dallas for believing in me no matter what. And I miss my mom.

To N, always my first and closest reader, to E and K for asking me what I'm doing and remembering the answer. To Ma for making me celebrate. I love you all so much.

And like we do when we learn that WE didn't do it, I thank God.

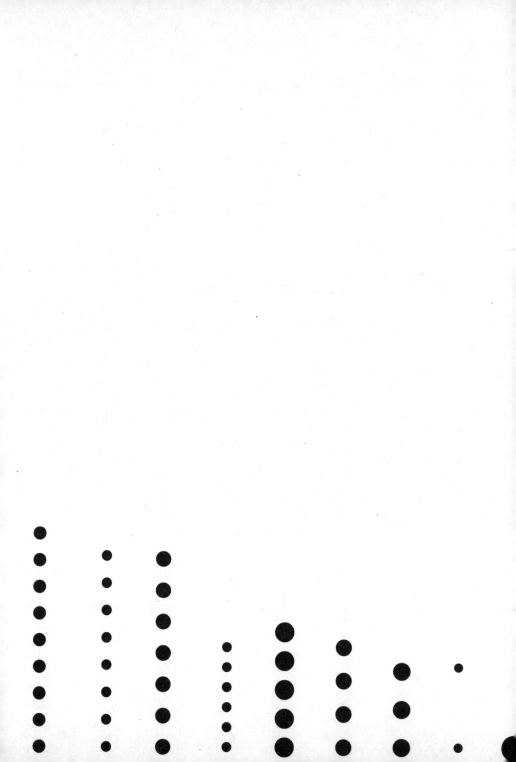

Douglas Kearney's collection of writing on poetics and performativity, *Mess and Mess and* (Noemi Press, 2015), was a Small Press Distribution Handpicked Selection that *Publishers Weekly* called "an extraordinary book." His third poetry collection, *Patter* (Red Hen Press, 2014) was a finalist for the California Book Award. *The Black Automaton* (Fence Books, 2009), was a National Poetry Series selection. *Someone Took They Tongues.* (Subito Press, 2016) collects three of his opera libretti. He was the guest editor for 2015's *Best American Experimental Writing* (Wesleyan). He has received a Whiting Writer's Award, residencies/fellowships from Cave Canem, the Rauschenberg Foundation, and others. Raised in Altadena, CA, he lives with his family in California's Santa Clarita Valley. He teaches at CalArts. www.douglaskearney.com